I0136344

More Praise for A Howling

From the howling coyotes in the opening poem, the poet signals a "goosebump flavor. . . quickening/ my steps toward home." Invoking over eighty species of fauna—ranging from mudskippers and triggerfish to chukars and civet cats to assassin bugs and the aardwolf—Blair's close observation and humor are on full display. But this is merely the backdrop to "the bare bone of lonely" when the poet braves the candid reflection of her life in poems like "Hounded": "I fondle/ my regrets." It is in these deeply personal poems that Blair's poetic power and her invocation of the animal world shine—when she homes in on the dark reality of her sister's illness: "pit viper/ coils/ in your pancreas,/ bites," how she "stood quailing" as a child in her father's presence, how familial relationships can be "as toxic as a scorpion." Conjuring Mary Oliver, we can only howl about Blair: "the soft animal of [her] body" has truly loved and lived.

—Cindy Williams Gutiérrez, author of *Inlay with Nacre: The Names of Forgotten Women*

a Howling

POEMS

SUSAN F. BLAIR

Press 53
Winston-Salem

Press 53, LLC
PO Box 30314
Winston-Salem, NC 27130

First Edition

A TOM LOMBARDO POETRY SELECTION

Copyright © 2023 by Susan F. Blair

All rights reserved, including the right of reproduction in whole or in part in any form except in the case of brief quotations embodied in critical articles or reviews. For permission, contact publisher at editor@press53.com or at the address above.

Cover image, "Trees Under Cloudy Sky Copyright © 2023 by Spencer Selover, Selover Designs
Licensed through Pexels

Cover design by Kevin Morgan Watson

Library of Congress Control Number
2023943536

ISBN 978-1-950413-68-3

"Death gives life meaning."

—Ludwig Wittgenstein

Contents

A Howling

Candle flame shudders
an act of bravery
in the dark.

Moon trolls shadows
lawn and tree
ghost-light.

Book tastes me,
spoons me over the landscape
of *Wuthering Heights.*

Sound shocks me upright,
licks my skin
with its goosebump flavor.

Coyotes—how many—

sweep the back yard,
yip-yip-yip-yip
their triumph of a kill

pure pleasure
for roaming wild and free
over moonlit terrain.

Walking home one night

I heard them howl,
who knows how close or far,
their signals bouncing off

our canyon walls, shivering
my spine, quickening
my steps toward home.

Book beckons. Walls hug me,
door whispers *I'm here,*
Heathcliff haunts the moors.

The Curse of the Gray Squirrel

I clamber up a ladder
of wisteria twined with arbor,
ignore the greening promise
of purple blossoms.

Sunflower seed lures me—
its aroma scoots me over boards
and branches to a feeder
full of toothsome gems.

I hang by my toenails
from the tube's chain
in full-body stretch,
reach for good eats.

On the ground below
a black cat paces
watches   waits
for me to fail.

I damn
its glowing eyes,
hurl a curse
on its furry head

for spooking me,
damn Audubon, too,
for its squirrel-proof claim
proven true.

I scramble back
up and over,
leap to an oak tree,
find an easy acorn.

Channeling David

Devils with feathers
bully the songbirds,
hog the seed tube,
suck up suet like
flying vacuum cleaners.

Invaders with locust zeal,
they sing gibberish,
parade the ground
without grace. Mary Oliver
would have me love

all the world,
but I am hatching
a black plot
to mimic David
with a sling:

not a murder
of crows
but of starlings.

So Good

water churns
        froth and foam
spillage tickles flowers

wings snap

body undulates
        glee
head neck back tail

punk-style feathers

male racy red
        can there be any
ecstasy

like a cardinal
        in a birdbath
unaware

of the cat below

I Yelp Over My Sister Donna's News

Her bleat fills the phone in my
ear—fake calm, as if to report
she's baking cookies—

stage   four   pancreatic   cancer

shock
no surprise

years of bellowing
at her husband for clothes
folded wrong, screeching

at her kids for carpeting
the floor with their Lego-
Lincoln Logs village, barking

at Mom for skipping
her meds, no respect
for her aging dementia—

she kneaded the dough
of her rage, rolled it
into a ball, stored it hot—

tumor rising in her belly.

The future stinks—
no more tales of dolphins
cruising with her kayak in Florida,

no more gifted bowls from
her potter's wheel, visits
with family in Buffalo empty

of her Pepsodent smile
and tomato quiche. I review
our claws-bared jealousy,

snarling about her tennis
trophies and boyfriends,
my privileges as Oldest Child

excellent grades—
the cream of our sisterhood
curdled by ice and fire,

days   weeks   months
when I hated her
for always having the last word,

weeks   months   years
of a sound-proof wall
after she declared me

as toxic as a scorpion
because I pushed back—
never a goddam apology—

I'll never have to
not
spit at her anymore.

Sigh, Writhe, Loathe

Ease of Adirondack chair,
green warmth of spring
like an arm around my shoulders,
scent of patio petunias
kisses my face.

Rustle in unraked leaves
pulls my eyes from my book.
Flash of white belly
against gray wall—
my neck-hairs salute the flag.

Two bull snakes create
their own Eden
in my garden—
hiss of the wild
under lilac tree—

thrash passion
make snake babies
goosebump my skin.
Stanley Kunitz praised
the wild braid

but I shudder
at these invaders,
this unholiness.

Run-on Sentences

I weed, prune, sweep
to the music of finches,
meadowlark from afar,
and this damned one-note

squawker with wings
who won't shut up.
This male house sparrow
cheepcheepcheeps non-stop,

at home on the neighbor's fence,
his bully pulpit, puffed up
like a preening politician
before a full house.

Maybe he's a proud papa
counting his nest eggs
as yet unhatched
and brag-worthy, or maybe

he's sounding the alarm,
under duress from climate
change or a cat, or claiming
territory. I want

peace, a cease-and-desist
order for this chatter
without end, without variety.
Get a job! Go catch bugs!

I screech at him,
last nerve twangs
learn another song!
I know people like this

who build walls of words
with no chink for breath,
with no room for another's
story.

The Smell of Money

Amid the green heat and humidity
of Ellendale, North Dakota,
I spent childhood summers
with Grandpa John and Grandma Nora,
farmers tough as bull rope.

One thousand acres where storms
rumbled like stampeding buffalo,
where windbreaks tamed the gusts
that raked the plain.

One thousand acres where they
raised corn and wheat,
cattle and chickens,
and one hundred pigs
that raised a big stink.

Grandpa, it really smells today
my nose protested.
Smile of pride from the pig farmer—
Honey, that's the smell of money.

Work the sacred word for every soul,
for farm dogs who guarded life and property
without dreams of a warm basket,
for farm cats who killed rodents
without hope of a thankful lap

(no paw allowed inside),
for me, who coddled
the hens with gentle baby-talk
while I collected their eggs,

for me, who trapped gophers,
anathema to agriculture,
bountied by the county
at ten cents a tail. First job, six
years old, I could keep the money.

Horrid prize one day—
civet cat trapped, gnarly and mad,
perfuming the air
with the stench of musk.

Who else could help
but Grandpa John, stomping
mad, irked to be called from work.
Rifle ready, one quick shot.
I saw the hole.

No money
for this tail.
No money
in this smell.

A Mudskipper Dishes the Dirt

Go ahead, call me Ishmael
cuz I'm one ishy fishy
slingin' the mud better than a politician.
You want a narrator? I got no classic tale
but here's a dirty story for you.

I'm a slimy kinda guy,
at home in the ooze,
build my burrow one mouthful
at a time, spit plugs of mud.

You see a fish out of water? That's me—
I live by land and by sea,
adaptable as hell, a fin in each country.

Ugly mug from somebody's genes—
pop-eyes on a flat head, wide mouth
set grim and grumpy—
but Mom wouldn't know me
from a hole in the dreck. She laid us eggs
then left us, left Dad to protect us
from a predator's jaws.

I wear my colors like a scuppernong,
greenish-bronze, but you won't confuse
us two. Check out my pectoral fins—
I can climb trees and low branches,
skip-to-my-Lou across the slop,
jump up and twirl, roll in the mud
to stay lubricated. The girls love it.
Then they love me, and we muck.

Reflections on Your Diagnosis

Your wheel of fortune spins
clicking, clicking, red, red,
lands on black,
loser.

Pit viper
coils
in your pancreas,
bites.

If you taste cayenne,
smell cesspool,
scream curses with all
your breath, I cannot know.

You do not share, do not
grant admission to the question.
Mom told me, once she found
you kneeling, beating your head

on the hardwood floor,
livid, impotent over Dad's
command: *apologize for your sass
or no college for you.*

Maybe you beat your head now
against the hard wood of chemo,
radiation, clinical trials at Hopkins—
like pouring Spanish gold doubloons

into the wishing well. Ye pays
yer money, takes yer goddam
chances, kicks that bucket
to hell.

How much time
can you bet against
viper venom. To hope
is just to lie.

Look

at the right moment
catch   a hummingbird

tiny jewel   singing wings
hovering   then

fire-flash   rocketing
into blue bliss   summer sky

look   ponder pleasures
of life   of this world

so quick

Navigators

They have slept in gravel beds,
shared shady pools,
known the caress of the current.

Ancient mariners,
salmon navigate
blue-green waters,

commune with Neptune
race with sea turtles
cavort with dolphins.

They have tasted the danger
of hook and line, jaw and claw,
chemicals and trash.

My sign is Pisces,
my birthstone aquamarine,
but I am no mission-minded swimmer.

They have endured a beating
spurred by the need to spawn,
as true to purpose as compass to north.

Home now in their Wenatchee River,
they lie fin to fin, as tired as mountains,
so thick I could walk across

on their backs. They offer
up their rotting bodies
to the furtherance of all,

feed the future with their pasts,
bridge life with death
with life again.

My Lesson

He swooped
from high above me
folded his enormity
hovered beside my
five-year-old height.

Chalk in hand
I stood quailing.

Playroom blackboard
beloved toy
yawned   like a remora.

No game this time.
Time for my lesson.

My father had heard
cackles   valentines
with wrong words.
He would catch me
in my backwardness,
my mistake prey
to his love   for correcting.

Write the word FROM.

His owl eye watched
for my error   chance
to snatch and feast
on my flaw.

I squirmed in the trap,
scrambled to escape
his claws.

Hand fluttered with dread
I printed *F O R M*
on the brutal blackboard.

Gleam in his eyes
curl of his lip
crow of triumph
at snaring my
failing.

I saw the shape
outlined in chalk
his love for me
would take.

His force would lurk
forever   to put my
letters   to put me
in my place.

Eagle Exemplar

Easy time
sky
under your wings

art of the glide
what crosses
your tiny mind

as you scan
the world below?
Prey?

No rocks in your path
to stumble
your steps

no mud
to suck you
into inertia

nothing chasing you
but the rush
of blue air.

Teach me
the art
of eagle Tai Chi

to live like you
a gift
to the sky.

My Sister Reclining, Declining

As determined as a chinook
swimming upstream,
she walked hard with me,

needs a lie-down now,
throws a woven shawl
over her sinking body.

I sit nearby, crochet away
the help my hands ache
to give, helpless here.

I gawk in secret at her
stick-arms, chicken legs,
derriere so little there,

signs that disease has thieved
forty pounds of flesh, a cruel
un-hexing of the family fat curse.

She drowses questions
from behind closed eyes.
I clip response, wait for sleep.

I love you, Susan—a shock—
her words an electric
eel from a deep cave.

Years of sibling warfare
melt into ground zero.
Our base.

I fake strength, steady
my voice with rare words—
I love you too, Donna.

She sinks into sleep,
jaw slack, shawl rising
and falling with each heartbeat.

Pale Frog, Pale Gripper

As likely as a falcon
with vertigo, this frog
in our semi-desert—

froglet, tiny jumper
could jitterbug
on my pinky fingernail

ghostly white, stuck
to my watering can's
interior wall

thrill of moisture
need of moisture
its life depends

on my
not shaking
to evict

When You Fell from the Sky

did it hurt?
You smacked the table
like a water balloon on pavement,
hijacked my eyes from my book.

Stunning fellow, elegant
in formal black, yellow stripes,
plump with fuzz, buzzless.
Your unmoving moves me—
are you stunned?

Once I watched your fellow bee
pillow on the purple cup
of a petunia, sweet repose,
as still as a classroom in summer.
Do you slumber, bumblebee?

The afternoon yawns.
You and I, still here, sunning.
Did you pass from that plummet?
Did a killer hornet stab you, steal
your gold, cancel your flight?

My eyes wander horizonward.
Breeze pats my cheek,
lilacs scent me, I crave honey,
look down again.
You are gone.

The Lion

There must have been other animals,
monkeys, for example,
with human-like eyes,
and elephants, great gray suitcases.
It's The Lion I remember.

The thrill so hot and bright
I held Dad's hand, skipped
my way to The Lion's cage.

I gawked at the great mane,
flicking tail, monster teeth
revealed in a yawn.

I stared at The Lion
he stared at me

I waited for a sign,
willed him to recognize me
from my visit a year ago,
wondered if lions ever forget.

Then—*Dad, he winked at me again!*
His smile, half-loving, half-knowing,
too amused and for once too kind
to shatter my crystal joy
with the truth.

Dad was king of our family with a roar
that could shiver the frame of our home,
shake the small bodies of his five children
prey to his mood swings.

As an adult I realized

how he had cut his way
through the jungle
of babies, bosses, bills
to climb his career.

At some point
our zoo visits stopped—
our family grew,
we grew up.

Sometimes I chatter to his gravestone—
Dad, remember the Lion
that always winked at me?

How to Live on Tenterhooks

The sun thrums five p.m.
Skin of our house twitches
like a wildebeest at a watering hole
wary of the crocodile's bite. Smell
of fear mingles with the aroma
of roast in the oven. Mom pours
her first bourbon-and-water, we kids
pore over our homework.
Each of us crosses the vast savannah
of wait and watch.

Garage door jaws snap open,
telegraph the signal *Daddy's home,*
time to sniff the air for calm or storm,
decide whether to run.

This is how, this is how I learned
how to live on tenterhooks.

Dwindling

Visitors mean   more stress
        than pleasure   she   wants   to   hide
            from everyone   from everything
curl into   a ball   hibernate   like a marmot
after the asteroid hit
burrow   into warmth   safety
for   sixty   million   years

she sits   stands   lies down   moves
lies down   doesn't move   sits   stands
aches   for comfort
        vomits   chemicals
tries   to gather   a thought   be clear

cries   hopes
tries to   hold on   to strength
shrinks   in the stare   of family
        witnessing   her life
sentence

Obscenity

My classmates
fourth-graders

roar glee and horror
over my misdeed.

Middle finger erect
between three curled fingers—

I mimicked the boy
with each hand. Easy

like rolling your tongue
into a tube in your mouth.

Fox-clever, I thought.
Eel-flexible, I thought.

Teacher's words whipped me
naughty girl nasty girl

stung

like hornets in my ears.
A nine-year-old girl

doesn't know
what she doesn't know.

I sit alone amid classmates,
their shun like sackcloth,

learn the obscenity
of killing a lesson.

After the Dinner Date

Yes, you were young and alone
in the city, your new home,
craving companionship,
ready for romance,

yes, he was German,
and to practice speaking it
meant a connection
which spoke to homesickness,

yes, you yielded
to his persistence
and rode with him
on that dinner date,

yes, you saw rape in the windshield
when he parked behind the warehouse
insisting *ein bisschen schmoosen ist doch normal,*
pawing like a German shepherd demanding treats,

and yes, those bruises bloomed purple
and you wanted to burn those clothes
and your teeth chattered
with the telling, the reliving,

but ah, my dear,
the woman we've become
knows you spoke the language
of escape with your calm.

Life

Like a youth sporting
his first whiskers

this young male struts
his twig-like antlers,

stalks my back yard,
noses dogwood tree,

nibbles rose leaves,
learns about thorns,

nudges bird feeders to lap
up seeds like a teen

raiding fridge and pantry,
hungry for everything.

Cougar Repast

Pardon my belch—
you were delicious,
paw-licking good.
I caught you unawares,
out-foxed you,
my success your demise,
you my dinner—*huzzah!*

Venison feast *al fresco*
rare raw catch of the day,
maybe of the week.
I pick fur from my teeth,
lick your juice from my face,
need a lie-down now,
sated, sleepy.

For Miss Manners I left
a leg bone on the trail.
Let the hikers gawk at it,
let them tread in trepidation,
ponder how I stalk
in padded silence, wonder
if I'll invite them for lunch.

Chemo Flows, But

pacing
in the shadows
keeping   its   distance

marking its territory
flexing   claws
pausing

yawning   maw
packed with teeth
there   can be   no   argument

licking paws   staring
yellow eyes
as old as   God

sleepless   beast
patient   beast
waiting

pacing
throaty   rumble
thrumming

like the long   low   note
of   bow   on   string
which may   break

at   any   time
pacing   waiting
panting

now   crouching
ready   to   spring

An Assassin Bug Reports on a Hit

My mouth parts, three sets—check.
Long rostrum assembled,
sharpness checked.
Terrain surveyed—
dirt, leaves, a coupla stones.
Good cover.
Vantage point scoped out,
position taken.
Antennae raised. Proboscis poised.

Mission of The Family—
Reduviidae—check.
Hungry for promotion.
Hungry.

Target spotted,
bumping along, guard down.
Thinks he has all day.

Think again, punk—
your guts are mine.
Closer, closer, enter the diner.
Victim arrives.
Say your prayers,
you lousy cockroach.

Exoskeleton stilettoed.
My hollow beak filled
with poison—check.
Injected. Lethal.
Victim's insides dissolved.
Asset liquidated—check.

My beak repurposed,
syringe now a straw—
check. Sucked up
cockroach soup for lunch.
Check.

A Risk of Lobsters

Time to migrate.
A few days' journey
across the lagoon floor.
Danger.

Nerves primed, antennae tuned,
we formed a conga line
claw to tail
to reduce water drag—

I got your back, you got mine.
Other lines joined, doubled
our caravan to sixty strong.
Swam-crawled at a good clip,

lobsters brisk, followed the current
toward ease of deep water.
Our geometry—line into circle
for defense against threats.

Like triggerfish.
Like the one that got Charlie.

Poor guy was out of line,
wanted to go solo too soon.

Triggerfish took aim,
clipped one antenna then
the other, left Charlie
clueless, chewed him

legless, left his shell
like a ragged old shoe.
We reached shelter,
rich reefs at edge of ocean

drop-off, on our own now,
safe from storms
churning waters high above,
riskless.

On the Way Through

April has rolled up
the white blanket of winter.

Tiny chocolate eggs
nestle in the grass, a sign

that deer passed through.
I mark their progress

across the lawn, wonder
at their copious droppings.

I wonder who will notice
when I have risen and walked

away, when the veil is lifted.

Living Room Window

They're falling away,
things she feels like doing,
sliding past like the Niagara River
she watches from her living room window.

She says she's poor company—
no stories, no critter reports except for sparrows
at the feeder hanging from the maple tree,
no jokes about this deadpan tumor.

The hospital gave her
a blood infection, then gave her
antibiotics, so she must avoid the sun,
take this ringside seat to boredom.

She can't get comfortable,
mass pressing on her abdomen,
end pressing on her life
as even the river gets old.

I see her
slipping away
as I look through my own
living room window.

In the Garden with Plato

I have disturbed
a worm. My pulling
grass and weeds
trespassing in my garden
has turned a worm
topside. It writhes
in the sun, then lies
corpse-like, shocked by air
devoid of moisture.

I weed, reveal
another worm, pink tip
peering from the dirt
like a subterranean periscope,
then it vanishes,
cringing from exposure
like a naked woman
in the window.

        I know the feeling
of being dug up, of being
forced into the glare of truth,
of wanting to crawl
back into my cave.

Harbinger

Is life worth leaving?
—James Joyce

1.
Darkness
quiet
she lies still.

Screeching voices
pick at her brain
like crows on carrion.

She plans to stay
wound in bed linens
take the dark fall.

Outside her window
a robin bugles breaking news:
Night Opens, Light Comes.

She pulls the sheet
from her face, tells the robin,
Wait, worm-eater, I will feed you.

Bottle on her nightstand
waits like a vulture
wings of the deep.

Darkness
her moment
now.

Banner of blank morning
hovers below the eastern clouds
waiting for a story.

Could she?

2.
Today, today, today the robin trills.
She flutters at his summons
like a fledgling.

Could she?

She unwinds the sheets
and reaches. The hollow
in the pillow

marks her flight

Diaspora

A narrow escape route—
this crack in the sidewalk
teems with ants, a seething crowd
of tiny black bodies forced overground.

No steady march this, no parade,
no trailing of comrades' scent,
no mission to collect the corpse
of a fallen beetle to feed the colony—

this is upheaval, this is loss,
this is mass panic in the face
of nestlessness. Did the tunnel
collapse under tyranny of the boot?

Did an atom-sized bomb
explode while they slept,
shatter walls and ceilings,
leave holes

in their homeland? Was there
time to grab their eggs
before flight? Now they must
emigrate across hostile concrete,

drag sacrifice like the carcass
of a grasshopper, seek refuge
in unknown terrain, seek
the language of dirt,

resettle, rebuild,
stare into the dark,
pray that
no aardvark looms.

When to Pray

After the horse is calm again
and the rattlesnake has crawled away,

after the machines have clicked
their pictures and the doctors
have seen his brain-shadow,

after the surgeons have drilled,
after the blood has pooled out,
after the questions have flown
from every direction,

after his dyslexia has flipped back
and his balance has normalized,
after the note on the bathroom mirror
reminds him daily of his name

because he must reconstruct his past
which hit the ground with his head
and fled into desert shadow
with the snake,

after the doctors have covered their asses
with *Give it time* and *No guarantees,*
after the vastness of loss
rears up at you,

after the hot breath
of *Oh please oh please oh please*
has ripped through the canyon
of your soul,

after you've reintroduced yourself
to God saying *yes,*
it's been a long time,
but could we overlook that for now

That Night

we flocked around your bed
like crows on a wire
watching and waiting,

black cello groaning
like an injured bear,
rising.

Your almost-closed eyes
grew wide as if dazed
by the invitation,

as if saying, *you mean now?*
and ready to accept
willing to accept
maybe glad to accept.

Your husband sobbed
your daughter shrieked
your son crumpled.

Leaden tongue
bitters in my throat
heart twisting

stale presence of old flowers
and damp bodies—
the cello moaned

*open the window—let
her spirit go,* but I knew

your spirit would haunt me,
whisper *Don't criticize me*
like a mosquito in my ear.

A Moment to Hold

1.
I sit on the patio
amid the green smell of lawn
and clear freedom of sky,
ready to taste the day.

A black body skims the blue,
glides on seasoned wings,
croaks a throaty greeting
to the morning.

A second raven follows,
shares the wealth of air
and altitude, joins in the joy
of trumping gravity.

House Sparrows gossip,
coarseness of jays the topic,
California Quail—Keystone Kops
of the bird world—dither about

with chukars chasing
and racing them like third-grade
boys bullying first-graders
at recess time.

2.
Like fog rolling in
a gray cat oozes
down the neighbor's rock wall
into my garden, slinks

through stalks of iris,
threads its way between rose bushes,
a tiny tiger in my jungle
of flowers and foliage.

I beckon with kissy sounds
but cat feigns deafness, parades
the pomp of *I'm ignoring you,*
struts past me as proof.

3.
Nature wraps itself
around me   my yearning
grows like a weed.
I crave someone's touch.

4.
As quick as a tail-flick
cat decides that social distancing
is for the birds, trots to me
with furry flag in full salute.

My touch makes purr makes
somersaults of ecstasy and cat,
with the power of whim,
jumps onto my lap for more.

5.
Allotted time spent, cat
hops down, moves two inches
beyond my reach, sniffs, licks
its fur, stalks off like a diva

leaving me alone again
with the flavor of belonging
like melted chocolate on my tongue
and gray fur on my black leggings.

6.
Cat returns, doubles my
surprise, drops a dead vole
at my feet, feasts on the gift
given and taken back.

My Bathrobe Speaks to Me

Oh,
the many times I've held you
in my arms, hugged you
more fully than your spouse,
settled arguments between you
and your cold house. I've
cocooned you in comfort,
soothed the sting of family
and friends as absent
as salamanders in snow.
I have collected your tears,
your sweat, your glee.
What you read, what you write,
what you dream embed in me.
We two turn trio
as your feline child claims
your lap, kneads your legs,
laps up your caresses.
Bits of her fur cling to me
like a tune caught in your head.
I wear her well. Cozy trinity,
we nestle and purr.
Purple and turquoise my colors,
you wear them well
like the bruises you hide.

A Deer in the Dark

Silhouette of hunger

against a backdrop
of town lights
blurred by fog

a deer picks its way
shoulder-deep in snow
across the yard.

Where is the apple
of hope
that will melt

this white world of longing

On the Feast of the Assumption of
the Blessed Virgin Mary, August 15

Pain
bit into her
a wolf chewing without relief
gnawing her sharp words
into soft moans
shaking her life
like a pit bull shakes
a rat.

Madame Morphine,
    Pain's partner in time,
        drooped her eyelids,
            slacked her jaw.

Through her fog
she lifted her arms
again and again, dropped
them like dead pheasants—
again and again
the lift and drop—
a plea for help or a hug,
or a reflex of resistance
against agony.

Without warning
she opened her eyes
wide as if amazed,
wide as if energized,
wide as if invited.
Then Pain left.

We howled
    a hollow hallelujah
        for so had she.

Sentinel

for my brother Mike, who was there

Five steps from bed to window—
you turn it into miles of back and forth,
mark-time-marching
because you can't sit still
under the wet wool blanket,
waiting for Dad to die.

You tried.
You were like a puppy
wriggling at possibility,
sitting up for Dad's praise,
fetching hope like a rubber ball.

You stay, as faithful as the question
of his belief in you, blood
of his blood, your marching
meshed with his heartbeat,
with his browbeating of you.

Five steps from bed to window,
one for each of us kids,
your throat pinching
at each turn,
watching him fail.

You walk and watch and walk and stay,
slip out once
for air and a beer
with a friend—
care for the caregiver.

Dad still has strength to spit in a glass,
Some Number One Son.

So you're there you're there you're there,
mind scraped numb by the hours,
trying to pray. Dad said,
Hail Marys don't work anymore.

Nor does
"Our Father who art in heaven."

You flanked his bed, watched
him frown, eyes empty as the windows
of our deserted home,
searching your face
for clues to *Number One Son,*
his prize after three daughters.

You turned to the window
one of hundreds of times,
turned back to the bed—
it was just an instant—
looked—
a tiny moment—
whispered to the nurse
he's not breathing—

her odd expression
as if, *what did you expect—*
you looked away
once too often.

That damned window.
He slipped past you
like a panther in the dark.

Ambivalence, Maybe

I sit astride
    this split-rail fence
ride it
    like a horse
taking me
    nowhere
pastureland
    spread around me
like an ocean
    of options
I waffle
    in the middle
teeter
    between stay
or go
    I don't know
what to do
    I do know
limbo
    New Year's
irresolution
    I pendulum
my leg
    over to ride
side-saddle
    side-step
decision
    were this a picket
fence
    I would
            jump

The Serpent Plans Another Prank on Eve

This   this surprise   I'd like

I'd uncoil myself   from my   rock
   where   I'd lie   all lummy and   yummy   in the sun
come   slimmering   slummering

glamor   in my   sleek   slinky   slide
     no stride   a glad-glanded glide
of lovely   leglessness   lovely   evil

now that you   know me
  you'd abhor my   slithery   glory
your loathing   slides a smile   across my face

you'd lie   under the tree   crave
  another   apple
I'd sneak   up the trunk   seek my limb

of whim   ooze drily   drape myself
   in leathery loops   drop   all ploppy
on your face

devout coward   you'd howl
beat feet   in retreat
   sweet

this   this surprise   I'd like

A Coypu Cops an Attitude

My orthodontist's wet dream,
enamel to envy—iron-fortified,
orange the new chainsaw,
jazz-jawed.

I scythe through reeds and rushes
fashion a floating raft
waft my way downriver
like Jim and Huck.

I rip up rhizomes, tear into tubers,
leave river plants without leaves,
chew through tires and wooden house
paneling without a belch. Badass me.

Chasin' tail? Catch mine—
long and skinny as a whip
hairless to a point—
point is, no rat, no muskrat here.

Want a coat like mine?
My fur: a pleasure, treasure
of trappers, foresight of fur farmers—
I'm a cultivated guy

not eager to be called *beaver.*
Though I play at water's edge,
dwell in dens partially submerged,
nutria my Spanish name

I ought to explain: I'm no otter.
You don't get it? Bite me.
Threaten me, human or dog,
I'll bite you back.

Bite me, eat me—here in the bayou
folks have for decades. Lean,
less cholesterol than beef—
ah, nutritious nutria,

fit for the whiskeyed
and the whiskered—you can
can me up for dogfood.
See you at midnight.

They Say That Funerals Are for the Living

Like a border collie
herding sheep, duty prods us.
Family and friends flock to our pews

to honor Donna
with prayers and Father O'Brien's
sugared words.

We speak in mouse-tones,
faces gray, clasping hands
to bridge the loss,

paying our respects—
as if she cares
about collecting the debt.

She lobbed her lemons,
dribbled her honey   we lick
salt off our cheeks.

What remains of her life—
a hole in her family,
shovels thumping in the dirt.

Breaking News

Chirpy, aka Camp Robber, member
of gang known as Stellar's Jays,
known thief of picnic treats,
killed Wednesday morning,
victim of apparent fly-by attack.

Suspect in custody, windowpane,
charged and found clean. Neighbors
trying to make sense of tragic loss
quoted: *Such a nice bird,*
would perch on your shoulder.
Sure could squawk. Wouldn't hurt
a fly—unless he was hungry.

Children came together, collected
shoebox, cotton, twigs and leaves
for burial. Memorial service
to be held Thursday after school.

In lieu of flowers,
please bring peanuts.

A Mockingbird Needs an Audience

Attend to me.
I am a bird
who apes.

I repeat all I hear,
pour all my juice
into any role.

Artiste, I sing
linguistics, every note
of any language—
> *chanson*
> *canzone*
> *das Lied*

aria after aria
opera coloratura—
how lyrical my life!

Soloist, diva,
I flaunt white wing
patches in flight—

my feather boa.
I hoard the limelight,
chase nightingales

from my stage.
I *vibrato*
for attention.

Bare Bone

Like a school hallway in summer,
like a tire swing heaped with snow,
like a birdfeeder without seeds,
I know *alone.*

Phone struck dumb,
mailbox yawning
with boredom,

I check email like a hawk
scanning the landscape
for quail, waiting for
the Godot of a message.

Former friendships skitter
across my memory, brittled
by the suck of *so busy.*

I suck the marrow from
the bare bone of lonely,
bend from the waist
into the wind of *forgotten.*

Grief, That Surprise Without a Party

It   hobbles   your   steps
   dis rupts   you   mid-sentence
     you   forget
  what   you   did   yesterday

It   wrings   you   dry
   stuffs up   your nose
puffs up   your eyes
  sucks up   your strength

It   sags   your   shoulders
  bows   your   back
turns your   legs
   to   Christmas tinsel

It   lurks
  a tiger   strike
    rips   your   throat
   words   bleed

Your Hands, Dad

I remember them
thick like German sausage,
gold band on the left ring finger,
Notre Dame class ring on the right,
nails groomed to godlike perfection.

I saw them
engulfing the cup
with thumb and forefinger
while chatting with me
and my dolls over tea.

I heard them
dipping fingertips
in talcum powder, hopping them
across the dining room table
around our Easter baskets.

I remember them
closing around mine
like oven mitts
to dance with me
standing on your feet.

I saw them
engraving your name
in black slants like ravens
of authority
on my report cards.

I watched them
wielding your tennis racket,
hoisting trophies
and bourbons
at the club,

I felt them
slapping my face,
Zeus hurling lightning
into my eyes, bitter brew
onto my tongue.

I watched them
lighting decades-long
chains of cigarettes,
flicking ash
and years away.

I see your hands, Dad,
lying on your chest
as empty as a broken promise,
arms crossed at the wrist
in your pine box.

Juggernauts

Flashing lights
trucks clustered
on the shoulder—

you can't help
looking
as you flash past

sixty miles per hour—
you can't
unsee

the deer
held by an ankle
hauled into the back

of a pickup
neck flopping
tongue lolling—

hurtling
down the road
picture seared

in your brain's
photo album—
sixty miles an hour

because we can

Hard Air

The *bonk* pulled me
from my chair to confirm
the hard truth
of sliding glass door.

Like a bobble-head toy
white-crowned sparrow
sprawls on the step.

Its right leg sticks
out like a cane, tiny eyes
flutter against the pain
of feeling the sky falling.

I reflect
upon hitting walls
while flying
through my career.

Bosses, editors smacked
me down, doors I closed
and locked against hard lessons
shocked me into inertia.

Sparrow stays stunned.
I plan a burial,
rehearse an elegy
of regret in my head,

take a step forward
to determine when last rites
for its last flight
will be in order.

Sparrow flies away.

I Know, I Know

Today as I arrive,
the first-grade classroom
is alive with sobs,
the kind that explode

from the toes
up through the body
like a tsunami
of grief.

Little Tommy flies
to my arms, gulps shake
his shoulders, tears soak
my shirt as he shares

a car   ran over   my dog Jasper

Oh, I know this pain.
I have grieved
five feline children,
last month a sister.

In the book of life
death has many chapters.
I know new suns coming
will burn away

these seven-year-old clouds,
but for now,
his pain, I know—
as big as he is.

I know
that a piece of this pain
will stick in him,
shape the pearl of his life,

that a distant star
in his night dreams
will shine on that jewel
of memory.

I know you will miss him,
I whisper, *I know, I know.*

Pockets Full of Ghosts

haunt me

turquoise tote   black straps
jaunty slant   on my shoulder
twin pockets
which steal my keys—

knapsack in orange-gold-cream cloth
matching zippered bag   nestled inside
like a joey in mama's pouch
to herd small items   keep them close—

too-large big shirt
wooden buttons   two breast pockets
fleece   to chase the chill
I wear it   like a hug—

giant bag   open-mouthed
like a basking shark   gobbles
my books and notebooks   clunks
with my overload   against my thigh—

proof   of fingers filled with skill
artifacts   of my dead sister's sewing talent
jump at me   from my closet   shelves,
yank sobs   from my chest

Greylock Bond

Artifact,
his stack of paper, tidy
in his desk drawer,
its brown sheath wrapping
torn and wrinkled
like a snakeskin shedding.

How taut,
rectangles of blue
and pink lines, poised
to take his measured words.

How tense,
authority of his hand
striding across the page,
scarring the sheet beneath.

How tight,
relic of his reign over
us in life, worm-smile
at us in death.

I play my childhood game,
hold the page to the light,
reveal the secret code:
"GREYLOCK BOND
An LLBROWN *paper.*"

I remember the lock-bond
of his punishments.

My father's stack of paper
waits in my desk drawer,
a tombstone
about to be engraved.

Proteles cristatus

From the Greek *protos* plus *teleos* I am,
complete in front with five-toed feet I am,
thick of neck and hunched of back I am,
from the Latin *cristatus* I am,
provided with a comb—my mane—I am,
long of leg and broad of tongue I am—
sticky tongue to lap up termites I have,
hundreds of thousands per night I can,
conserver of their mounds I am,
planner of future meals I am,
I am woman, hear me laugh
when I find food—
stalker of the night I am,
sleeper in day-burrows I am,
roamer of bush and plain I am,
matriarch of the pack I am,
loaded with testosterone I am,
out-aggress any male I can,
defender of the social order I am—
high intelligence I have,
hideous beauty I have—
aardvark I am
not, werewolf I am
not, from the Afrikaans
earth wolf I am,
I am
aardwolf.

Room to Room

Scent of old roses lingering
in her last exhale follows me
wherever I grieve.
I see her in bed fading,
body gnawed to bone,
a ghost-to-be. I force
myself to breathe
without sobs or tears
to make room for sleep,
which will not come,
which will not come,
which will not come.
Door shut, windows closed,
I hear breathing not my own
as steady as a hibernating bear—
Donna breathing
good-bye.

Hounded

Like a litter
of golden retrievers
wriggling, climbing
all over me,
licking my face,
giving me their soft
bellies to rub,
chewing my shoelaces,
biting my fingers,
peeing in my lap,
I fondle
my regrets.

Black Widow Spider Soliloquies

Scene I
I, Claudius   creep   woodpile hamlet
Gertrude   queen   of my heart   rules my loins
throne of silk   her corset   begs   my undoing
red hourglass chimes   time for sex

Scene II
My body listens   for twang   on web
enter   a Lothario   eight-legged swagger
cocksure   I take his lust   in stride
he'll rue his greed   my juice   secret herb
no   grace   in   my   love

Scene III
Her feast-fragrance   siren song
safe sex beckons   desire desire desire
I share   my treasure
relic   of future   generations

Scene IV
The play's the thing   I'll foil   his fun
I lie   I consumed nothing   before Claudius
came   no second consummation
in this court   no encore
for this act

Scene V
Horatio   I die
Horatio   I dine

Notes

"Channeling David"

The poet Mary Oliver (1935-2019) wrote about her sense of wonder with all of nature. She won the Pulitzer Prize in 1984 and the National Book Award in 1992.

"Sigh, Writhe, Loathe"

Stanley Kunitz' poem, "The Snakes of September," appears in his book, *The Wild Braid.*
Part of it reads:
> "At my touch the wild
>   braid of creation
>   trembles"

"An Assassin Bug Reports on a Hit"

The Reduviidae is a large cosmopolitan family of the order Hemiptera. Almost all species are terrestrial ambush predators.

"A Coypu Cops an Attitude"

The nutria (Myocastor coypus), also known as the coypu, is a large, herbivorous, semiaquatic rodent. It has large incisors that are yellow to orange-red on the outer surface, a result of stain from iron in the tooth enamel. "Jim and Huck" refers to the characters in Mark Twain's *Huckleberry Finn.*

"*Proteles cristatus*"

The aardwolf is an insectivorous species of hyena, native to East and Southern Africa. Its name means "earth-wolf" in Afrikaans and Dutch. It resembles a very thin striped hyena, but with a more slender muzzle, black vertical stripes on a coat of yellowish fur, and a long, distinct mane down the midline of the neck and back.

My sister, Donna Kay Finney Brownschidle (1958-2019), died of pancreatic cancer eighteen months after her diagnosis.

Acknowledgments

"When to Pray," *Spank the Carp*, 2023

"Hard Air," *San Pedro River Review*, Fall 2022

"Chemo Flows, But," *Spillway 29*, 2021 (Tebot Bach)

"My Bathrobe Speaks to Me," *From Whispers to Roars*, July 2020, in a
slightly different version

These poems appeared in an earlier chapbook, *What Remains of a
Life* (Finishing Line Press, 2018), in a slightly different version:

"My Lesson"
"Greylock Bond"

Many thanks to my editor, Tom Lombardo, for his generous time,
attention, and guidance in putting this collection together, and to my
publisher, Kevin Morgan Watson and Press 53, for making this book
a reality.

Susan F. Blair is the author of *What Remains of a Life*. Her poems have appeared in *Spank the Carp, San Pedro River Review, Spillway 29, From Whispers to Roars,* and others. She founded and edits *The Shrub-Steppe Poetry Journal*. She has written a series of *Perri the Poetry Fairy Presents Poems for Kids,* which she presents in costume. Monthly, she writes the "Poetry Matters" column for *The Good Life* magazine and hosts the "Third Thursday Poets" open mic. She earned a BA in German and Russian from Middlebury College.

www.ingramcontent.com/pod-product-compliance
Lightning Source LLC
Chambersburg PA
CBHW021509090426
42739CB00007B/546

9781950413683